KT-444-541

Usborne Activities

Dinosaur Quizzes

Sarah Khan

Illustrated by Sarah Horne

Designed by Kate Rimmer, Joanne Kirkby
and Candice Whatmore

Edited by Phil Clarke
and Sam Taplin

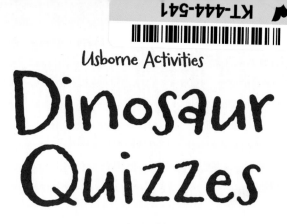

What are dinosaurs?

(1) **Dinosaurs were:**

    a) reptiles   b) amphibians   c) mammals

(2) **The time when the dinosaurs lived is divided into three periods. Which of these is NOT one of them?**

    a) Jurassic

    b) Triassic

    c) Herbaceous

(3) **How many types of dinosaurs have been identified and named so far?**

    a) around 70

    b) over 700

    c) over 7,000

(4) Did any dinosaurs live in the sea?

(5) For roughly how many million years did dinosaurs exist?
   a) 16   b) 65   c) 165

(6) When did dinosaurs first appear on the planet?
   a) around 2 million years ago
   b) around 25 million years ago
   c) around 250 million years ago

(7) The word 'dinosaur' means:
   a) very loud lizard
   b) awe-inspiring lizard
   c) enormous lizard

Tyrannosaurus rex

Tyrannosaurus rex was a fierce predator that lived around 85 to 65 million years ago. It was one of the largest meat-eating dinosaurs that ever lived.

(1) **What is the only place where *Tyrannosaurus* fossils have been found?**

a) Asia   b) Europe   c) North America

(2) ***Tyrannosaurus* was the biggest meat-eating dinosaur of all.**
True or false?

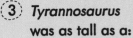

(3) ***Tyrannosaurus* was as tall as a:**

a) crane

b) tractor

c) double-decker bus

(4) ***Tyrannosaurus* was as heavy as a:**

a) car   b) bus   c) plane

5 *Tyrannosaurus rex* was the only type of tyrannosaur. True or false?

6 Roughly how many teeth did *Tyrannosaurus* have?
a) 16   b) 60   c) 160

7 A teenage *Tyrannosaurus* went through a growth spurt. How much weight did it put on every week?
a) 1.5kg (3lbs)
b) 15kg (33lbs)
c) 150kg (330lbs)

8 The name *Tyrannosaurus rex* means:
a) giant royal lizard
b) prince of the meat-eaters
c) tyrant lizard king

9 *Tyrannosaurus'* biggest teeth were the size of:

a) almonds   b) bananas   c) cucumbers

10 Using its strong neck muscles, what size animal could a *Tyrannosaurus* have tossed into the air like a pancake?

a) cat

b) sheep

c) horse

11 Did *Tyrannosaurus* have poor vision or excellent eyesight?

12 *Tyrannosaurus'* little two-fingered arms were too puny to be of any use.

True or false?

13 The scientist who discovered, in 1900, the first parts of a *Tyrannosaurus* skeleton was named:

a) Barnum Brown

b) Graham Greene

c) Penuel Pink

Sauropods

Sauropods were a group of huge plant-eaters with bulky bodies, small heads and long necks and tails. The biggest and the least intelligent dinosaurs belonged to the sauropod family.

1 **The largest sauropod brain was no heavier than:**
a) an apple
b) a grapefruit
c) a watermelon

2 *Europasaurus* **was a sauropod that was only the size of a:**
a) bull
b) rhinoceros
c) elephant

3 **Scientists used to think that sauropods lived under water:**
True or false?

4 *Sauroposeidon* **was tall enough to peer into the top window of a:**
a) three-floor building
b) six-floor building
c) nine-floor building

(5) Sauropods may have walked on four legs but run on two legs.
True or false?

(6) This is *Mamenchisaurus*. Humans eat roughly 2,000 calories a day. How many did it eat?

a) 1,000
b) 10,000
c) 100,000

(7) For how many million years did the sauropods survive on the Earth?

a) 4   b) 140   c) 800

(8) Which of these is the name of a real sauropod whose fossils were found near a famous river?

a) *Fujisaurus*
b) *Kayakasaurus*
c) *Amazonsaurus*

9 *Brachytrechalopan* had a long name, but the shortest what of any sauropod?

a) tail   b) neck   c) legs

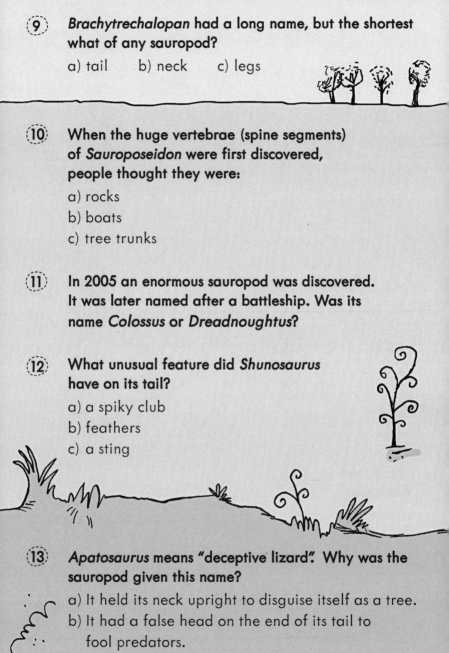

10 When the huge vertebrae (spine segments) of *Sauroposeidon* were first discovered, people thought they were:

a) rocks
b) boats
c) tree trunks

11 In 2005 an enormous sauropod was discovered. It was later named after a battleship. Was its name *Colossus* or *Dreadnoughtus*?

12 What unusual feature did *Shunosaurus* have on its tail?

a) a spiky club
b) feathers
c) a sting

13 *Apatosaurus* means "deceptive lizard". Why was the sauropod given this name?

a) It held its neck upright to disguise itself as a tree.
b) It had a false head on the end of its tail to fool predators.
c) Its discoverer thought that its tail bones looked just like the tail bones of a giant sea reptile.

Diplodocus

Diplodocus was a huge, plant-eating sauropod that lived between 155 and 145 million years ago. It had a small head, and a long neck and tail.

(1) **Diplodocus' brain was the size of a person's:**
a) toe   b) fist   c) head

(2) **Was *Diplodocus'* neck longer or shorter than a giraffe's?**

(3) **Diplodocus' tail was the length of how many boa constrictor snakes?**
a) 1
b) 4
c) 8

(4) **Diplodocus' front legs were much shorter than its back legs.**
True or false?

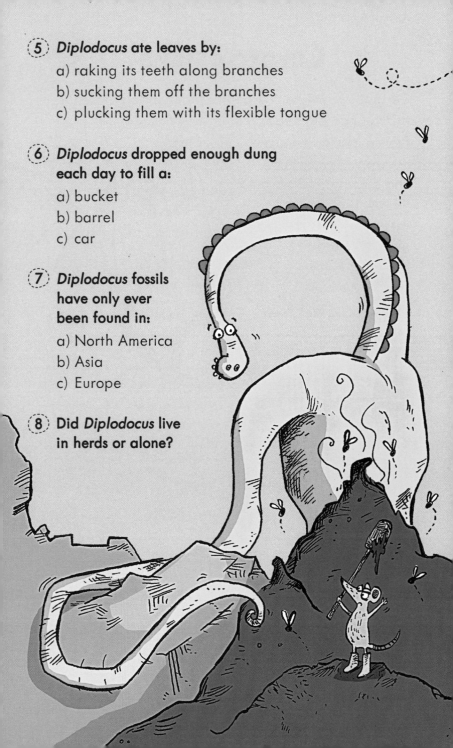

5) *Diplodocus* ate leaves by:

a) raking its teeth along branches
b) sucking them off the branches
c) plucking them with its flexible tongue

6) *Diplodocus* dropped enough dung each day to fill a:

a) bucket
b) barrel
c) car

7) *Diplodocus* fossils have only ever been found in:

a) North America
b) Asia
c) Europe

8) Did *Diplodocus* live in herds or alone?

Ceratopsians

Ceratopsians were a group of plant-eating dinosaurs that all had big heads and horns, frills around their necks, and walked on four legs.

1. **This dinosaur is _Einiosaurus_. It used its downward-curving horn to:**
   a) pick up food
   b) scratch itself
   c) defend itself

2. **Were ceratopsians' neck frills made of bone or muscle?**

3. **Which of these is NOT a real ceratopsian?**
   a) _Ojoceratops_
   b) _Jojoceratops_
   c) _Mojoceratops_

4. **_Triceratops_ was the biggest ceratopsian.** True or false?

(5) These little dinosaurs are *Archaeoceratops*, some of the smallest ceratopsians. They were only twice the size of a:

a) hamster   b) cat   c) pony

(6) Were male ceratopsians' frills and horns usually larger or smaller than females'?

(7) All ceratopsians were born with similar-shaped heads, and they only developed their different horns and frills as they grew older.
True or false?

(8) One type of ceratopsian had bony, snake-like growths around its neck frill. Was this dinosaur called *Medusaceratops* or *Sphinxceratops*?

Triceratops

Triceratops was a plant-eating, rhinoceros-like ceratopsian with three horns on its face and a bony frill around its neck. It lived between 72 and 65 million years ago.

1) *Triceratops* lived in...

    a) wetlands   b) rainforests   c) deserts

2) Was a *Triceratops* two, four or six times larger than a rhino?

3) What was the toughest thing a *Triceratops* could chew through?

    a) leaf   b) tree trunk   c) rock

4) How many teeth did *Triceratops* have?

    a) 80
    b) 800
    c) 8,000

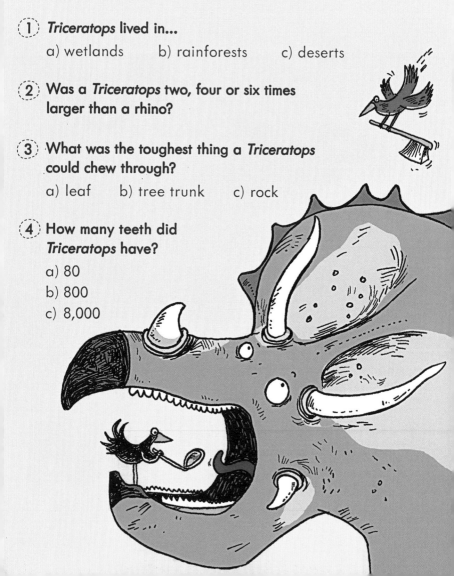

5. *Triceratops* is thought to have used its neck frill for which two of these purposes?

a) to reflect sunlight into predators' eyes
b) to control its body temperature
c) to attract mates

6. The horns above *Triceratops'* eyes were as long as:

a) bowling pins   b) golf clubs   c) surfboards

7. *Triceratops* weighed as much as a:

a) car
b) truck
c) tank

8. Male *Triceratops* locked horns to fight over females.
True or false?

25
50
100

Stegosaurs

Stegosaurs were a group of plant-eating dinosaurs with rows of plates and spikes along their backs and sharp spikes on the ends of their tails.

1) **About how many bones did this stegosaur, _Miragaia_, have in its unusually long neck?**

a) 7   b) 17   c) 77

2) **Stegosaurs' teeth were shaped like:**
   a) leaves
   b) pegs
   c) daggers

3) **Could stegosaurs run quickly?**

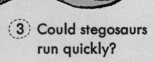

4) **Did stegosaurs use their back plates to defend themselves from attack?**

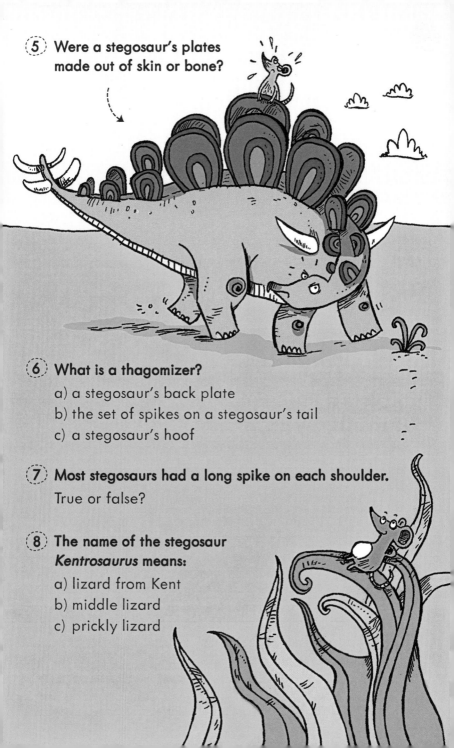

5 Were a stegosaur's plates made out of skin or bone?

6 What is a thagomizer?
   a) a stegosaur's back plate
   b) the set of spikes on a stegosaur's tail
   c) a stegosaur's hoof

7 Most stegosaurs had a long spike on each shoulder. True or false?

8 The name of the stegosaur *Kentrosaurus* means:
   a) lizard from Kent
   b) middle lizard
   c) prickly lizard

Stegosaurus

Stegosaurus was a small-brained, plant-eating stegosaur that lived between 156 and 140 million years ago. It had big, triangular plates along its back, and a heavy, spiked tail.

1. **The name *Stegosaurus* means:**
   a) walled lizard   b) roofed lizard   c) floored lizard

2. **Only male Stegosauruses had plates on their backs.**
   True or false?

3. **Were *Stegosaurus'* back legs the same length as its front legs?**

4. ***Stegosaurus* is most likely to have used the plates on its back for which two of these purposes?**
   a) to control its body temperature
   b) to attack other dinosaurs
   c) to tell its own kind from other stegosaur species

5 The older a Stegosaurus became, the more tail spikes it grew.

True or false?

6 In which two of these continents have *Stegosaurus* fossils been found?

a) Europe   b) Asia   c) North America

7 Running at top speed, *Stegosaurus* could move as quickly as the world's fastest:

a) lawnmower   b) sprinter   c) bicycle

8 Although *Stegosaurus* was bigger than an elephant, its brain was only the size of a:

a) strawberry   b) lemon   c) coconut

Dromaeosaurs

Dromaeosaurs were a fierce, meat-eating group of dinosaurs that walked on two legs and had long claws, which they used to kill their prey. They were closely related to birds, and had feathers.

1. **Dromaeosaurs are nicknamed:**
   a) raptors   b) dinobirds   c) slashers

2. **Did dromaeosaurs slash their victims with the claws on their fingers or the claws on their toes?**

3. **Did some dromaeosaurs hunt in packs or did they all hunt on their own?**

4. **The most intelligent dinosaur ever found was a dromaeosaur.** True or false?

5) Scientists think that the turkey-sized dromaeosaur *Saurornitholestes* may have fed on the giant pterosaur *Quetzalcoatlus* because:

a) pterosaur bones were found in its stomach

b) its tooth was found stuck in the pterosaur's leg bone

c) close relatives are known to have hunted pterosaurs

6) The heaviest dromaeosaur, *Utahraptor*, was how many times heavier than the lightest dromaeosaur, *Microraptor*?

a) 5　　b) 50　　c) 500

7) Dromaeosaurs were so intelligent, you could train them to sit, roll over and shake hands, just like dogs.

True or false?

Velociraptor

Velociraptor was a vicious, meat-eating dromaeosaur. It had sharp claws and teeth, and lived in hot, dry places around 85 to 80 million years ago.

1. Could Velociraptors have jumped onto the backs of bigger prey to attack them from behind?

2. Were *Velociraptor*'s teeth smooth or jagged?

3. Which was more intelligent – *Velociraptor* or *Tyrannosaurus rex*?

4. Could Velociraptors grow as tall as human adults?

(5) Did Velociraptors use their feathers to help them fly?

(6) The Velociraptors shown in the Hollywood movie 'Jurassic Park' were actually based on another type of dromaeosaur, known today as:
   a) *Microraptor*
   b) *Atrociraptor*
   c) *Deinonychus*

(7) Which would Velociraptors NOT eat?
   a) fish
   b) rotting flesh
   c) other Velociraptors

(8) Could Velociraptors have used their claws to pull out their victims' intestines?

Ankylosaurs

Ankylosaurs were a group of plant-eating dinosaurs that were covered in tough, protective scales, spikes and bony plates. Some had clubs at the end of their tails, which they swung at approaching predators.

1. Did any ankylosaurs have more than one club at the end of their tail?

2. The novel 'Jurassic Park' by Michael Crichton inspired the name of an ankylosaur. What was it?
   a) *Michaelsaurus*
   b) *Jurasaurus*
   c) *Crichtonosaurus*

3. Did any ankylosaurs have plated eyelids?

4. Ankylosaurs are nicknamed:
   a) plated dinosaurs
   b) tank dinosaurs
   c) shield dinosaurs

S-m-ash

5) Ankylosaurs sometimes hit things so hard with their tails that their tail clubs broke off.
True or false?

6) Did *Ankylosaurus* sweat a lot, or break wind a lot?

7) *Euoplocephalus* was so well covered by plates and spikes, that the only way for a predator such as *Tyrannosaurus* to injure it would be to:
a) slash at its one unprotected ankle
b) flip it onto its back and dig into its soft belly
c) pierce the patch of bare skin under its chin

8) The ankylosaur *Antarctopelta* was remarkable because:
a) it had no teeth
b) its large feet worked like snowshoes
c) it was the first dinosaur to be found in Antarctica

Hadrosaurs

Hadrosaurs were a group of gentle, plant-eating dinosaurs that had thick, short bodies and tough beaks. Many hadrosaurs lived together in large herds.

1. **What does the name 'hadrosaur' mean?**
   a) bulky lizard
   b) tall lizard
   c) gentle lizard

2. **What could hadrosaurs not bend: their tails or their legs?**

3. **Hadrosaurs, like this *Lambeosaurus*, fed their babies by swallowing food, then vomiting it up for them.**
   True or false?

4. **Did *Tyrannosaurus* hunt hadrosaurs?**

5 Some hadrosaurs used the crests on their heads to:

a) make sounds to communicate
b) blow out gas from their bodies
c) sneeze through

6 Giant hadrosaur *Shantungosaurus* weighed as much as:

a) 10 lions   b) 10 elephants   c) 10 blue whales

7 Hadrosaurs grazed on four feet but may have run away from predators on two feet.

True or false?

8 How long did it take a baby hadrosaur to grow into an adult?

a) less than 6 years
b) 8–12 years
c) over 16 years

Paaarp

Pachycephalosaurs

Pachycephalosaurs were a group of plant-eating dinosaurs with thick skulls. They walked on two legs, and may have roamed in herds.

1. **What does the name 'pachycephalosaur' mean?**
   a) dome-headed lizard
   b) bone-headed lizard
   c) thick-headed lizard

w-h-ack

2. **Why may pachycephalosaurs have head-butted each other?**
   a) as a form of greeting
   b) to fight for dominance in their herd
   c) to warn others of danger

3. **Were pachycephalosaurs' skulls so big because they housed huge brains?**

4. ***Stygimoloch*** **is a pachycephalosaur whose name means:**
   a) pig monster from the lake of tears
   b) horned devil from the river of death
   c) black slug from the swamp of despair

5. The most commonly found pachycephalosaur fossil is of which part of its body?
   a) its leg
   b) its tail
   c) its skull

6. The thickest part of a *Pachycephalosaurus* skull was as thick as how many bricks?
   a) 2   b) 4   c) 6

7. Which was the biggest pachycephalosaur of all?
   a) *Pachycephalosaurus*
   b) *Alaskacephale*
   c) *Stegoceras*

8. Which of these, inspired by J.K. Rowling's tales of Harry Potter, is the name of a real pachycephalosaur?
   a) *Norbertodon hagridia*
   b) *Basilisk voldemortia*
   c) *Dracorex hogwartsia*

Early birds

Most dinosaur scientists believe that birds are a type of dinosaur, and that they evolved from small meat-eaters. The first birds lived alongside dinosaurs.

1 **Did all prehistoric birds have teeth?**

2 **The giant, flightless prehistoric bird *Bullockornis* was named after movie star Sandra Bullock.**

True or false?

3 **Which of these is one of the oldest known birds?**

a) *Seniopteryx*
b) *Archaeopteryx*
c) *Geriapteryx*

4. This penguin-like early bird is called *Hesperornis*. Did it use its feet more for diving or for walking?

5. *Ichthyornis* was the first early bird to be found with:
   a) teeth
   b) feathers
   c) eggs

6. The prehistoric bird *Archaeopteryx* was more likely to have:
   a) nested in trees
   b) nested on the ground
   c) nested on rocky ledges

7. Which of these is the name of a real prehistoric bird?
   a) *Jumbopteryx*
   b) *Gargantuavis*
   c) *Enormornis*

8 The early bird *Pengornis* got its name because:

a) it looked like a penguin

b) it was named after the Peng, a giant bird in Chinese legends

c) its fossil feathers looked like antique quill pens

9 In 2014, scientists announced a new discovery about *Archaeopteryx.* What was it?

a) it was blue

b) it had four wings

c) its legs were clothed in feather 'shorts'

10 A South American bird called the hoatzin has chicks that are like prehistoric birds because:

a) they have teeth

b) they have long, bony tails

c) they have claws on their wings

11 Which early bird, found in China, was named after a famous philosopher?

a) *Confuciusornis*

b) *Aristotleavis*

c) *Platopteryx*

12 *Pelagornis* was the biggest seabird ever, and possibly the biggest flying bird. How wide was its wingspan?

a) 3.7m (12ft)

b) 7.3m (24ft)

c) 14.6m (48ft)

Dinosaur names

1. Is the dinosaur *Camelotia* named after a camel or after King Arthur's legendary court, Camelot?

2. Which of these is the meaning of the dinosaur name *Megapnosaurus*?
   a) good happy lizard
   b) small hungry lizard
   c) big dead lizard

3. There is a dinosaur, *Eiffelosaurus*, named after the Eiffel Tower in France.
   True or false?

4. This beaked dinosaur is *Anatosaurus*. What does its name mean?
   a) duck lizard
   b) wading dinosaur
   c) water monster

5. This dinosaur is called *Zupaysaurus*, which means 'devil lizard'. Did it get its name because it looked like a devil, or because it was discovered in a place called Devil's Creek?

6. Which of these is a real dinosaur?
   a) *Irritator*
   b) *Botherer*
   c) *Infuriator*

7. The name of small, feathered dinosaur *Rahonavis* means:
   a) 'fear from the rivers' fish
   b) 'danger from the trees' lizard
   c) 'menace from the clouds' bird

8. *Eoraptor lunensis* is one of the earliest known dinosaurs. Its name means:
   a) night stalker from the Volcano of the Sun
   b) dawn thief from the Valley of the Moon
   c) dusk vandal from the Forest of the Stars

9 **All dinosaur species have two-part names, like _Tyrannosaurus rex_. Match these dinosaurs to the second parts of their names:**

Triceratops   longus
Velociraptor   horridus
Diplodocus   mongoliensis

10 **How did the early long-necked dinosaur _Vulcanodon_ ('volcano tooth') get its name?**
a) its fossil was found, with some teeth, between two ancient lava flows
b) its teeth had hollow tips, like volcanoes
c) it had big teeth and a hot temper

11 **Which of these is a bird-like dinosaur, named after a creature from a nonsense poem by Lewis Carroll?**
a) _Grinchia_
b) _Borogovia_
c) _Gruffalodon_

12 **The dinosaur _Gasosaurus_ was named after the gas-mining company that found the quarry where its fossil lay.**
True or false?

13 **Which of these dinosaurs was discovered in Africa?**
a) _Antarctosaurus_
b) _Malawisaurus_
c) _Koreaceratops_

Dinosaur giants

(1) **Which was the largest dinosaur?**
a) *Amphicoelias*
b) *Supersaurus*
c) *Diplodocus*

(2) **One of the biggest dinosaurs is known as 'The King of the Jurassic'. Is it** *Allosaurus* **or** *Tyrannosaurus*?

(3) **Which dinosaur was the biggest of the meat-eaters:** *Spinosaurus* **or** *Velociraptor*?

(4) *Argentinosaurus* **was a giant plant-eating dinosaur. Where were its fossils first discovered?**
a) Europe
b) South America
c) Asia

5) Which of these is the name of a real dinosaur giant?

   a) *Giraffatitan*   b) *Rhinotitan*   c) *Elephantitan*

6) *Mamenchisaurus* was a long-necked plant-eating dinosaur. It could grow to be as heavy as how many rhinos?

   a) 3   b) 10   c) 20

7) *Shantungosaurus* was a giant duck-billed dinosaur. It was the biggest animal ever known to:

   a) walk on two feet
   b) climb trees
   c) fly

8) The sea creature on the right is called *Shonisaurus*. Its eyeballs were as wide as:

   a) DVDs
   b) large pizzas
   c) car wheels

Tiny dinos

1. *Parvicursor* was a small dinosaur with long, slender legs that helped it to run quickly. Its name means:

   a) tiny foot   b) fast lizard   c) small runner

2. Some dinosaurs were only as long as matchsticks.

   True or false?

3. These little lizard-eating dinosaurs are Compsognathuses. They were around the size of a:

   a) hummingbird
   b) pigeon
   c) chicken

4. Is there a small dinosaur named after Disney's cartoon deer, Bambi?

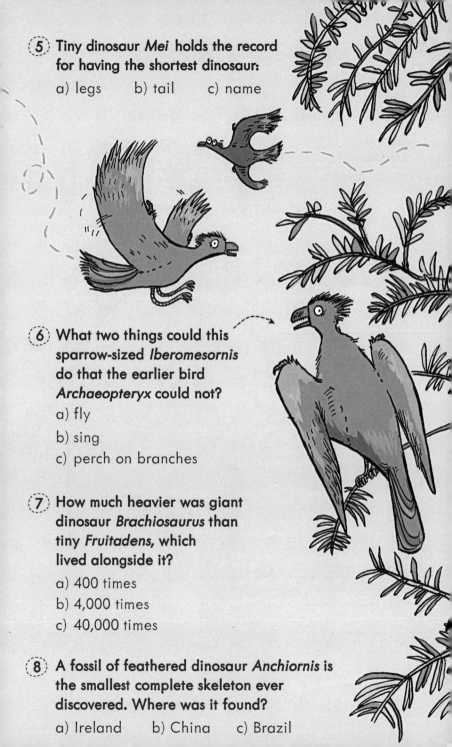

5 Tiny dinosaur *Mei* holds the record for having the shortest dinosaur:

a) legs   b) tail   c) name

6 What two things could this sparrow-sized *Iberomesornis* do that the earlier bird *Archaeopteryx* could not?

a) fly

b) sing

c) perch on branches

7 How much heavier was giant dinosaur *Brachiosaurus* than tiny *Fruitadens*, which lived alongside it?

a) 400 times

b) 4,000 times

c) 40,000 times

8 A fossil of feathered dinosaur *Anchiornis* is the smallest complete skeleton ever discovered. Where was it found?

a) Ireland   b) China   c) Brazil

Meat-munchers

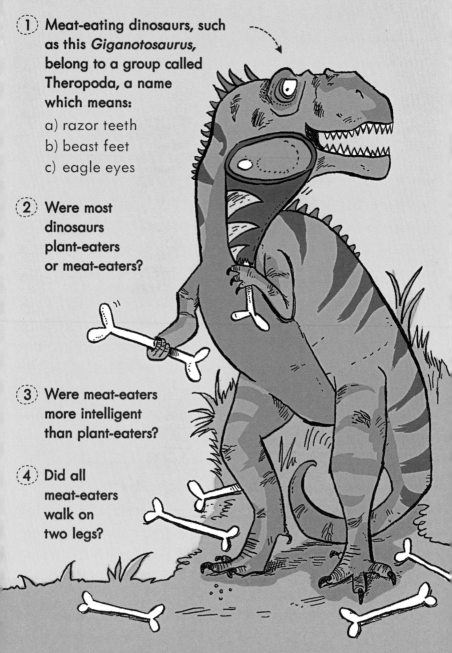

1. Meat-eating dinosaurs, such as this *Giganotosaurus*, belong to a group called Theropoda, a name which means:
   a) razor teeth
   b) beast feet
   c) eagle eyes

2. Were most dinosaurs plant-eaters or meat-eaters?

3. Were meat-eaters more intelligent than plant-eaters?

4. Did all meat-eaters walk on two legs?

5 Have more fossils been found of injured meat-eaters or injured plant-eaters?

6 Did any meat-eating dinosaurs have straight claws?

7 This giant dinosaur is a *Saurophaganax*. It was one of the largest meat-eating dinosaurs in North America. The name *Saurophaganax* means:

a) best of the lizard-hunters
b) fastest of the lizard-chasers
c) king of the lizard-eaters

8 All meat-eaters had three toes on each foot.

True or false?

Plant-eaters

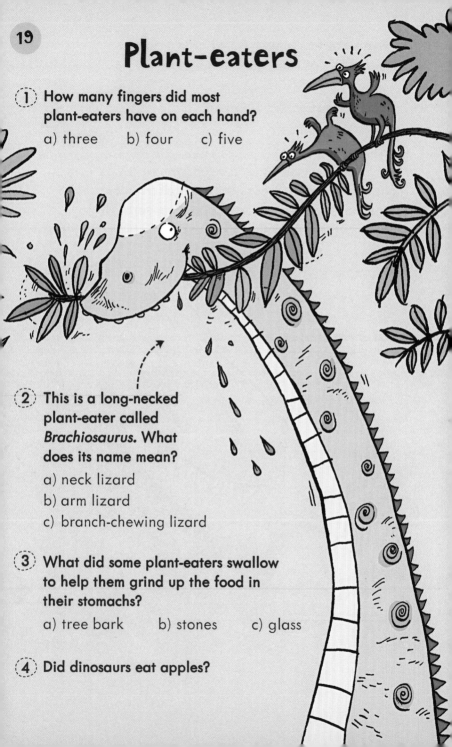

1) How many fingers did most plant-eaters have on each hand?

a) three   b) four   c) five

2) This is a long-necked plant-eater called *Brachiosaurus*. What does its name mean?

a) neck lizard
b) arm lizard
c) branch-chewing lizard

3) What did some plant-eaters swallow to help them grind up the food in their stomachs?

a) tree bark   b) stones   c) glass

4) Did dinosaurs eat apples?

5) Which of these plant-eaters was the only one that could move its jaws up, down and sideways when it chewed?

   a) *Hadrosaurus*
   b) *Diplodocus*
   c) *Triceratops*

6) Did any of the plant-eaters have sharp fangs?

7) *Nigersaurus* had a wide mouth, like a hippo. How did it eat plants?

   a) it sucked them up like a vacuum cleaner
   b) it sliced them up like a pair of shears
   c) it mowed them down like a lawnmower

8) Hadrosaurs, such as this *Edmontosaurus*, ate mainly fruit.
   True or false?

Eggs and nests

1. **This is *Hypacrosaurus*. It laid some of the largest known dinosaur eggs. How big were they?**

   a) the size of a melon
   b) the size of a car wheel
   c) the size of a person

2. **The first dinosaur egg fossils were found in 1869 in which country?**

   a) China
   b) Canada
   c) France

3. **Were all dinosaur eggs the same shape?**

4. **Some dinosaurs laid their eggs in water.**
   True or false?

(5) A dinosaur could lay up to how many eggs in a year?
   a) 50   b) 100   c) 150

(6) Which of these dinosaurs sat on their eggs to keep them warm?
   a) hadrosaurs
   b) oviraptorosaurs
   c) stegosaurs

(7) Were all dinosaur eggs smooth or were some covered in wrinkles and bumps?

(8) Some dinosaurs nested in colonies, building hundreds of nests in the same area.
   True or false?

BIG BOOK OF BABY NAMES

Babies and youngsters

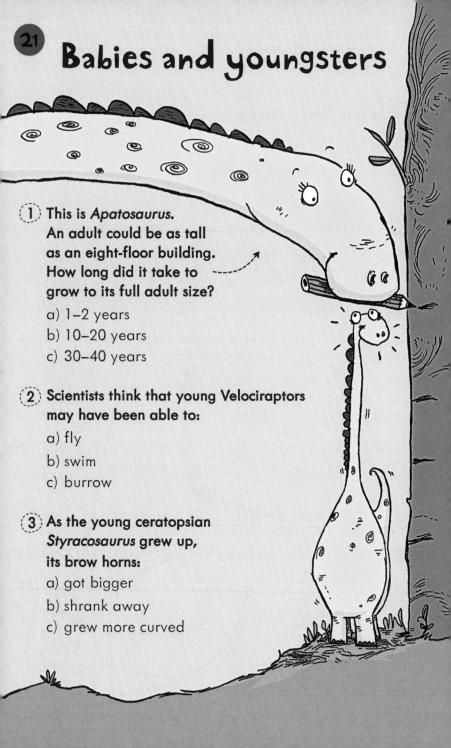

1. This is *Apatosaurus*.
   An adult could be as tall
   as an eight-floor building.
   How long did it take to
   grow to its full adult size?
   a) 1–2 years
   b) 10–20 years
   c) 30–40 years

2. Scientists think that young Velociraptors
   may have been able to:
   a) fly
   b) swim
   c) burrow

3. As the young ceratopsian
   Styracosaurus grew up,
   its brow horns:
   a) got bigger
   b) shrank away
   c) grew more curved

(4) Young tyrannosaurs may have been covered in chick-like fluff to keep them warm.
True or false?

(5) This is a flying reptile called a pterosaur. Young pterosaurs are known as:

a) flaplings b) dactylets c) wingsters

(6) Adult ankylosaurs were covered in bony plates. Baby ankylosaurs had plates that covered all parts of their bodies, except for their:

a) heads b) backs c) legs

(7) Did a young tyrannosaur eat the same foods as its parents?

Walking and running

1. Did dinosaurs usually walk on their toes or were they flat-footed?

2. If *Diplodocus* didn't keep at least three feet on the ground at all times, it would topple over.
   True or false?

3. This is a *Podokesaurus*. It was a small, fast-moving dinosaur. What does its name mean?
   a) swift-footed lizard
   b) lightning speed runner
   c) racing demon lizard

4. Which were usually faster: meat-eaters or plant-eaters?

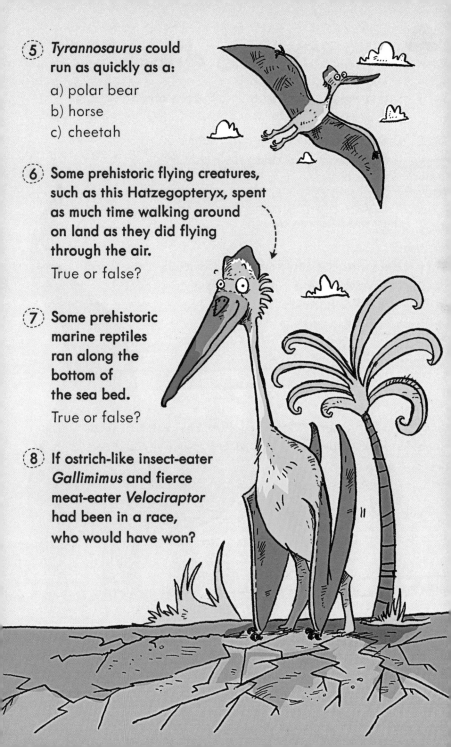

5) *Tyrannosaurus* could run as quickly as a:

a) polar bear
b) horse
c) cheetah

6) Some prehistoric flying creatures, such as this Hatzegopteryx, spent as much time walking around on land as they did flying through the air.

True or false?

7) Some prehistoric marine reptiles ran along the bottom of the sea bed.

True or false?

8) If ostrich-like insect-eater *Gallimimus* and fierce meat-eater *Velociraptor* had been in a race, who would have won?

Fighting dinos

1. Did teenage tyrannosaurs fight each other in gangs?

2. Did any dinosaurs hold their victims in a tight 'death grip' using their claws?

3. Is it likely that any dinosaurs kicked their predators to death?

4. *Ankylosaurus* could fracture the skull of *Tyrannosaurus* with a swing of its mighty tail club.

   True or false?

Clunk

5 In 1971, a fossil was found that showed a Protoceratops locked in deadly combat with a Velociraptor. How are they thought to have died?

   a) they fought until they died of exhaustion
   b) another dinosaur came along and killed them both
   c) they suffocated when a sand dune collapsed on top of them

6 Some dinosaurs had pig-like tusks that may have helped them fight off predators.
   True or false?

7 Did any dinosaurs spit venom to defend themselves from predators?

8 Did *Tyrannosaurus* prey on *Stegosaurus*?

Dinosaur world

1 Which of these prehistoric time periods is the oldest
and which is the most recent?

   a) Triassic   b) Cretaceous   c) Jurassic

2 In the middle of the Jurassic period, the Earth
had two continents. One was called
Gondwana; the other was:

   a) Laurasia
   b) Ellafrica
   c) Annamerica

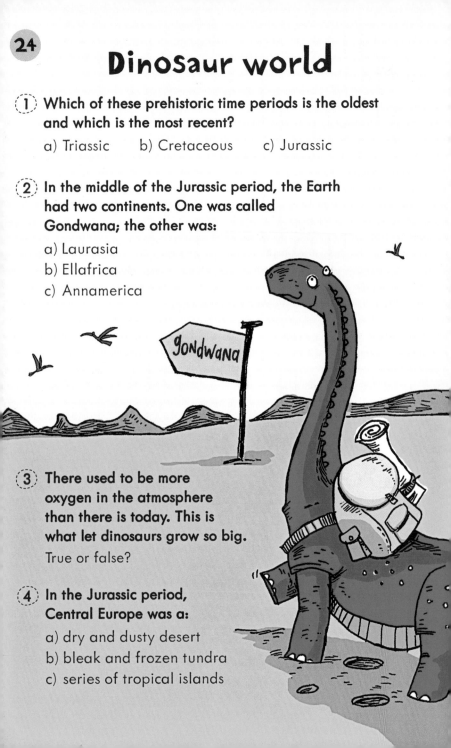

3 There used to be more
oxygen in the atmosphere
than there is today. This is
what let dinosaurs grow so big.
True or false?

4 In the Jurassic period,
Central Europe was a:

   a) dry and dusty desert
   b) bleak and frozen tundra
   c) series of tropical islands

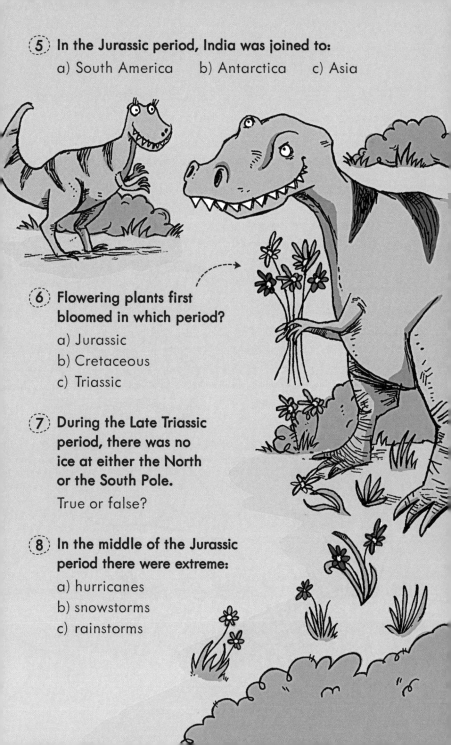

5 In the Jurassic period, India was joined to:

a) South America   b) Antarctica   c) Asia

6 Flowering plants first bloomed in which period?

a) Jurassic
b) Cretaceous
c) Triassic

7 During the Late Triassic period, there was no ice at either the North or the South Pole.

True or false?

8 In the middle of the Jurassic period there were extreme:

a) hurricanes
b) snowstorms
c) rainstorms

Head to head

1. A fossil of a small freshwater reptile named *Hyphalosaurus* discovered in China had two heads. True or false?

2. Some meat-eating dinosaurs had one eye that was bigger than the other. True or false?

3. Did any dinosaurs have nostrils in their foreheads?

4. The dinosaur on the right is *Tylocephale*. It had a very high and wide forehead. Its name means:
   a) dome lizard
   b) swollen head
   c) long face

5 There is a dinosaur with a name that means 'knuckle head'. True or false?

6 The dinosaur below is *Torosaurus*. It had the longest head of all the dinosaurs. Its head was as long as a:

    a) baseball bat   b) double bed   c) tank

7 *Gallimimus* was an ostrich-like dinosaur that had a strong beak. In which two ways may it have used its beak to find food?

    a) to crack open the eggs of other dinosaurs
    b) to cut leaves from branches
    c) to dig little animals out of mud

8 The huge sea reptile *Liopleurodon* had jaws strong enough to crush a car. True or false?

Terrific teeth

1. Flying reptile *Pterodaustro* had more than 1,000 teeth. True or false?

2. Long-necked plant-eating ancestors of *Diplodocus* had teeth shaped like:

   a) knives   b) forks   c) spoons

3. Most dinosaurs had lots of different types of teeth. True or false?

4. This buck-toothed dinosaur is an *Incisivosaurus*. Is it more likely to have used its big front teeth for biting prey or for gnawing plants?

5 Some meat-eating dinosaurs used small twigs to pick bits of flesh from between their teeth.

True or false?

6 This giant sea reptile is *Elasmosaurus*. How did it use its long, splaying teeth?

a) to chew its food
b) to trap and stab its prey
c) to inject venom into its prey

7 Did all dinosaurs have teeth?

8 Match these dinosaur names to their meanings:

Astrodon	wounding tooth
Troodon	star tooth
Deinodon	terrible tooth

Neck and neck

1. This is *Mamenchisaurus*. It had the longest neck of all the dinosaurs. Its neck was half as long as a:

   a) bus   b) tennis court   c) swimming pool

2. Some dinosaurs had no necks at all.
   True or false?

3. Dinosaur scientists once thought that long-necked *Barosaurus* had hearts in its neck to help pump blood to its brain. True or false?

4. For which two reasons did long-necked sauropods have hollow bones?

   a) to aid their blood circulation
   b) to lighten their enormous necks
   c) to help them breathe more easily

5 Did all plant-eating dinosaurs have long necks?

6 *Stegosaurus* had bony plates covering all the parts of its body, except its neck.
True or false?

7 This is *Amargasaurus*. It had two rows of spiny sails along its neck which it flapped up and down to keep cool.
True or false?

8 Most long-necked dinosaurs were born with short necks, which lengthened quickly as they grew older.
True or false?

Arms and legs

1. This desert-dwelling dinosaur is called *Mononykus*. What is it most likely to have used its long legs for?
   a) jumping over sand dunes
   b) wading in pools of water
   c) running quickly away from predators

2. Which dinosaur had stumps instead of fingers?
   a) *Velociraptor*
   b) *Saltasaurus*
   c) *Pteranodon*

3. How many working fingers did tyrannosaurs have?
   a) 2   b) 4   c) 6

4. Which dinosaurs had arms so small they were probably useless, dromaeosaurs or abelisaurids?

5 What did the bird-like maniraptoran dinosaurs do with their long arms when they ran?

   a) they tucked them close to their body
   b) they flapped them up and down
   c) they swung them to and fro

6 *Brontomerus* was a big, plant-eating dinosaur with very wide legs. What does its name mean?

   a) thick ankles
   b) knobbly knees
   c) thunder thighs

7 Meat-eaters' limbs were more muscly than plant-eaters'.
   True or false?

8 Did any dinosaurs leave horseshoe-shaped footprints?

99..100..

Dino claws

1. Is there evidence to suggest that dinosaurs kept their claws sharp by scratching them down tree trunks?

2. Did *Velociraptor* have longer claws on its fingers or on its toes?

3. If a dinosaur broke a claw, would a new one grow to replace it?

4. This is *Therizinosaurus*, the dinosaur with the longest claws. Its claws were roughly as long as a:
   a) jumbo hot dog
   b) golf club
   c) javelin

clip clip

5 Could dinosaurs draw their claws into their toes, like cats do?

6 Long-legged, turkey-sized dinosaur *Mononykus* is thought to have used its long, single claws for:
   a) spearing small mammals
   b) digging burrows
   c) tearing into rotten wood

7 Which flying reptile used its claws to clamber up trees and cliffs?
   a) *Dimorphodon*
   b) *Pteranodon*
   c) *Iguanodon*

8 This is *Baryonyx*. It used its claws to spear fish. What does its name mean?
   a) heavy claw
   b) fishing fingers
   c) spearing lizard

A dino's tail

1. *Stegosaurus* had spikes on the end of its tail.
   True or false?

2. Which dinosaur had the longest tail?
   a) *Velociraptor*
   b) *Apatosaurus*
   c) *Diplodocus*

3. This is *Leaellynasaura*.
   It lived near the South Pole
   and may have used its long
   tail to keep warm – but just
   how long was its tail?

   a) as long as its body
   b) three times as long
   c) six times as long

4. *Epidexipteryx* was a small
   bird-like dinosaur with four very
   long ribbon-like tail feathers. What
   do scientists think it used them for?

   a) for grabbing insects to eat
   b) for whipping predators
   c) for showing off to
      other dinosaurs

5. Most dinosaurs would have tipped head over heels if they didn't have a tail for balance.
True or false?

6. This is *Nomingia*, a human-sized dinosaur that looked like a cross between a turkey and a peacock. Do scientists think it used its fan-like tail to attract a mate or to keep cool?

7. *Rhamphorhynchus* was a flying reptile. What shape was the end of its tail?
a) club   b) diamond   c) spade

8. Which of these groups of dinosaurs had bony clubs at the end of their tails?
a) troodontids   b) ankylosaurs   c) maniraptors

Skin, scales and spikes

1. This little Chinese dinosaur is *Sinosauropteryx*. It was the first dinosaur known to be covered in:

   a) feathers
   b) fur
   c) wool

2. Did dinosaurs have dry or slimy skin?

3. The outlines of the bumps, scales and feathers of dinosaurs' skin have been found preserved in:

   a) wood   b) shells   c) rocks

(4) **The small gliding dinosaur *Microraptor* had:**
a) two wings   b) four wings   c) six wings

(5) ***Kulinadromeus* is a small, downy dinosaur whose discovery excited scientists for which TWO reasons?**
a) it was not a close relative of birds
b) it had scales and a downy coat
c) it had tall plates on its back

(6) **Which of these dinosaurs had porcupine-like quills on its tail?**
a) *Psittacosaurus*
b) *Stegosaurus*
c) *Tyrannosaurus*

(7) **Did dinosaurs' skin become wrinkled in old age?**

(8) **The skin of titanosaurs was covered in bony scales. Did these grow harder or softer as they grew older?**

Look-alikes

1) This is *Anchiornis*. It had a red crest on its head. Was this crest feathery like a woodpecker's, or fleshy like a hen's?

2) Small, plant-eating dinosaur *Kangnasaurus* was so named because it had a long tail, like a kangaroo's. True or false?

3) *Carnotaurus* was a long-necked, meat-eating dinosaur with very small arms and two horns on its forehead. What does its name mean?
   a) small-armed ram
   b) meat-eating bull
   c) long-necked antelope

4) *Psittacosaurus* had a short, sharp beak that it may have used to crack open nuts. Did this dinosaur look more like:
   a) an owl   b) a parrot   c) an ostrich

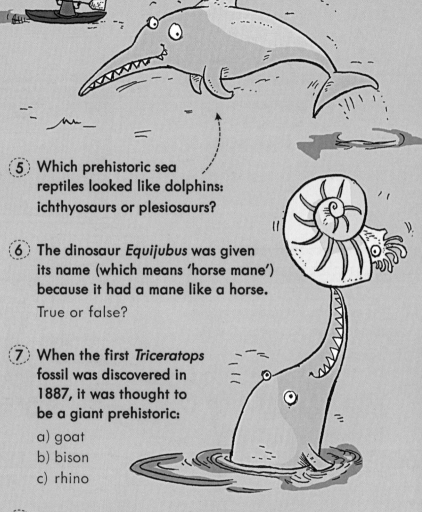

(5) Which prehistoric sea reptiles looked like dolphins: ichthyosaurs or plesiosaurs?

(6) The dinosaur *Equijubus* was given its name (which means 'horse mane') because it had a mane like a horse.

True or false?

(7) When the first *Triceratops* fossil was discovered in 1887, it was thought to be a giant prehistoric:

a) goat
b) bison
c) rhino

(8) *Dromiceiomimus* was a fast-moving, big-brained dinosaur. Its name means 'emu mimic' and it was so named because:

a) it had big eyes and long legs
b) it flapped its wings when running
c) it had dull brown, shaggy feathers

Dinosaur family tree

Dinosaurs are part of a larger group of reptiles called archosaurs. One type of archosaur is the ancestor of dinosaurs. Other types didn't evolve into dinosaurs, but did live alongside them.

1. **What does the name 'archosaur' mean?**
   a) first lizard
   b) ruling lizard
   c) ancestor lizard

2. **Are pterosaurs (flying reptiles) a type of archosaur?**

3. **The archosaur *Poposaurus* was named after Pope Pius the Tenth.** True or false?

4. **As well as dinosaurs, archosaurs are also the ancestors of which one of these animal groups?**
   a) crocodiles
   b) mammals
   c) snakes

DISTANT COUSIN CLIFFORD

ANCIENT AUNT AUDREY

GREAT GREAT GREAT GREAT GREAT GREAT GREAT GREAT GREAT GREAT GREAT GREAT UNCLE BARTIE

5 The archosaur below is called *Desmatosuchus*.
In which two ways did it use its long shoulder spikes?

a) for defending itself from predators

b) for impressing other archosaurs

c) for killing prey

6 The name of the archosaur
Batrachotomus means:

a) frog-slicer

b) beetle-crusher

c) lizard-swallower

7 Scientists tell archosaurs apart by looking at which
part of their remains?

a) tail

b) teeth

c) ankle

8 The name of the archosaur *Saurosuchus* means:

a) king crocodile

b) lizard crocodile

c) bird crocodile

34

Walking with dinosaurs

1. Which of these little creatures has NOT been found fossilized in dinosaur droppings?

   a) snail   b) dung beetle   c) fly

2. Did people live at the same time as dinosaurs?

3. The biggest mammals that lived alongside dinosaurs were the size of:

   a) hamsters   b) foxes   c) horses

4. Snakes evolved around 90 million years ago. The earliest snakes all had rattles at the end of their tails.

   True or false?

5 The crocodile below is *Sarcosuchus*, a creature that lived around 110 million years ago. How much longer was it than the largest modern crocodile?

a) two times   b) three times   c) four times

6 *Cretotrigona* is the oldest prehistoric bee found so far. Which of these things could it not do?

a) see   b) sting   c) fly

7 Komodo dragons, the biggest of today's lizards, lived alongside dinosaurs and may have eaten their eggs.

True or false?

8 Which of these animals didn't exist at the same time as dinosaurs?

a) frogs
b) bats
c) butterflies

SPOT A CROC

35

Australian dinosaurs

1. **Australian dinosaurs carried their young in pouches.**
   True or false?

2. **Which of these is NOT a real Australian dinosaur?**
   a) *Qantassaurus*
   b) *Ozraptor*
   c) *Koalasaurus*

3. **In the Early Cretaceous period, Australia was still joined to:**
   a) Asia
   b) Africa
   c) Antarctica

4. **The most complete fossil of a meat-eating dinosaur found in Australia was nicknamed what?**
   a) 'Hugh' after actor Hugh Jackman
   b) 'Banjo' after poet Banjo Paterson
   c) 'Kylie' after pop singer Kylie Minogue

5 The big plant-eater *Muttaburrasaurus* probably had large, inflatable nose sacs. What would they NOT have been used for?

a) making loud, honking sounds
b) giving a powerful sense of smell
c) firing sticky mucus at predators

6 110 million years ago, a large part of central Australia was covered by what?

a) a desert
b) a forest
c) a shallow sea

7 *Minmi* was a small Australian ankylosaur that was remarkable for its:

a) long horns
b) tiny brain
c) tail club

8 Lark Quarry in Queensland, Australia, has the world's largest number of what?

a) cave paintings of dinosaurs
b) fossilized dinosaur tracks
c) fossilized dinosaur eggs

9 Which of these was a real, fast-running, hunting dinosaur from Australia with slashing claws?

a) *Australovenator*
b) *Speediraptor*
c) *Scarisaurus*

36

Flying reptiles

Pterosaurs were flying reptiles that lived at the same time as the dinosaurs. They could fly long distances using their thin (but strong) wings.

1. This is *Hatzegopteryx*, one of the largest pterosaurs. It had the same wingspan as a:
   a) large bat
   b) large bird
   c) small plane

2. Did parent pterosaurs have to teach their young how to fly?

3. Were pterosaur eggs hard like birds' eggs or soft and leathery like crocodiles'?

4. Did pterosaurs have feathers?

5 The name 'pterosaur' means:

a) sky lizard   b) winged lizard   c) bird lizard

6 This flamingo-like pterosaur is *Pterodaustro*. It used its bristly teeth to:

a) trap flying insects
b) sift sand to catch sand bugs
c) filter tiny creatures
    from water

7 Which of these is NOT the name of a real prehistoric animal: *Pterodactyl* or *Pteranodon*?

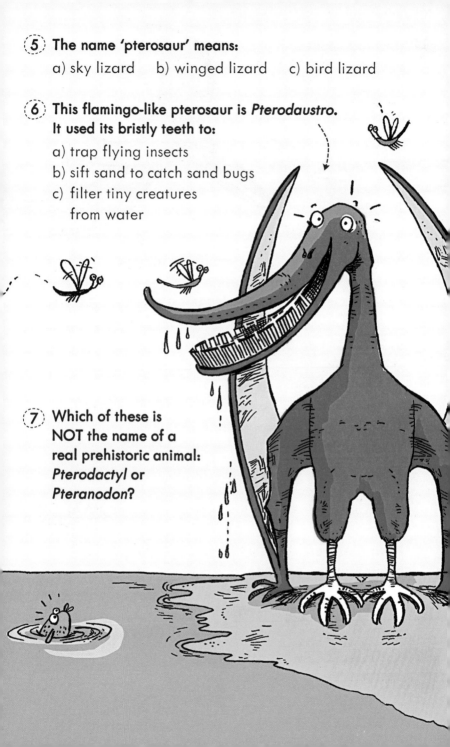

8 **How fast could pterosaurs fly?**

a) 75km/h (45mph)
b) 120km/h (75mph)
c) 250km/h (155mph)

9 **All pterosaurs had teeth.**

True or false?

10 **How do scientists think the biggest pterosaurs took off?**

a) They ran along the ground, flapping their wings.
b) They jumped off cliffs and floated on air currents.
c) They sprang off the ground, pushing with their back legs and strong arm muscles.

11 **The pterosaur *Nyctosaurus* had an unusual crest. Which of these is NOT a true fact about it?**

a) it was shaped like an antler
b) it was longer than its body
c) it used it to spear fish

12 **Pterosaurs were excellent fliers, but were nearly helpless on the ground.**

True or false?

13 **The giant pterosaur *Hatzegopteryx* had a beak large enough to swallow a:**

a) seagull
b) dog
c) man

37

Sea Creatures

1. Are prehistoric sea reptiles officially classed as dinosaurs?

2. The giant prehistoric fish *Leedsichthys* was how many times as long as a crocodile?
   a) 2   b) 3   c) 5

3. This giant prehistoric crab is called:
   a) *Giganzaclaurus*
   b) *Megaxantho*
   c) *Crustitan*

Snap!

4. In which two ways was prehistoric sea crocodile *Metriorhynchus* different from crocodiles today?
   a) it had no teeth
   b) it had flippers
   c) it had a shark-like tail

5 Fossils of the giant, long-snouted sea reptile *Polycotylus* have been found with what inside them?

a) nuts and berries   b) unborn babies   c) seals

6 A bone from which type of fish was found stuck between the teeth of a fossilized *Spinosaurus*?

a) sawfish   b) goldfish   c) jellyfish

7 Woodlouse-like creatures called trilobites scuttled along the ocean floors during the time of the dinosaurs.

True or false?

8 This is a giant sea turtle called *Archelon*. Its shell was as big as a:

a) car
b) tank
c) truck

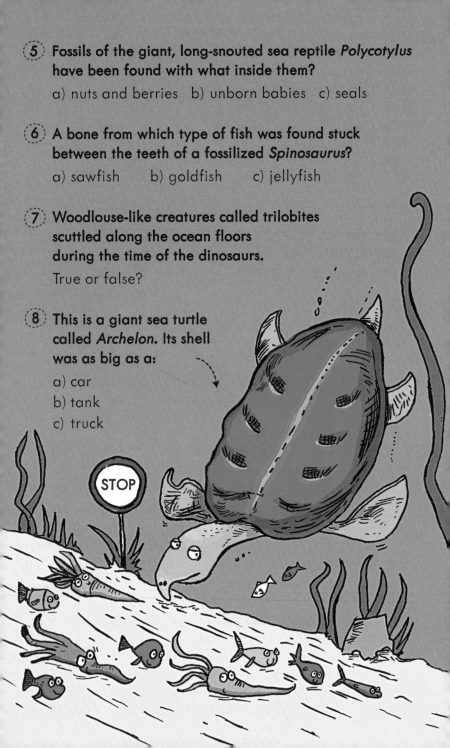

STOP

9. The long-necked sea reptile *Cryptoclidus* had jutting, needle-like teeth. How did it feed?

a) it tore chunks of flesh from other sea reptiles
b) it trapped fish and squid in its toothy jaws
c) it combed the seabed for shellfish

10. Pliosaurs were big, fierce sea reptiles with flippers and crocodile-like heads. The largest belonged to a group called the thalassophoneans. What does it mean?

a) sea slayers
b) huge hunters
c) blood seekers

11. The fossils of long-necked sea reptiles show that they often swallowed stones. Scientists think they did this for several reasons. Which of these is NOT one of them:

a) to help balance their bodies under water
b) for the important minerals inside them
c) to help grind up their food

12. Which of these sea creatures did NOT live at the same time as the dinosaurs?

a) squid
b) sharks
c) dolphins

13. The ichthyosaur (dolphin-like sea reptile) *Shonisaurus* was the biggest sea reptile of all time. Was it as big as a blue whale?

38

Nicknames

1. Due to its huge size and its heavy skull, prehistoric sea crocodile *Dakosaurus* is nicknamed:

   a) 'Godzilla'   b) 'Gremlin'   c) 'Bigfoot'

2. What kind of dinosaur was 'Big Al', a near-complete skeleton discovered in Wyoming, USA in 1991?

   a) *Gallimimus*   b) *Allosaurus*   c) *Megalosaurus*

3. *Cryolophosaurus* is nicknamed ⸻ 'Elvisaurus' because of its:

   a) curled upper lip
   b) swivelling hips
   c) head crest in the shape
      of a quiff hairstyle

4. The largest, most complete, and best-preserved *Tyrannosaurus rex* fossil ever discovered is nicknamed what?

   a) 'Bonecrusher'
   b) 'Firestorm'
   c) 'Sue'

5 *Anzu*, a 3m (10ft) tall feathered oviraptorosaur is nicknamed what?

a) 'Big Bird'
b) 'the chicken from hell'
c) 'the terrible turkey'

6 'Bone heads' is the nickname of which group of dinosaurs?

a) ceratopsians
b) tyrannosaurs
c) pachycephalosaurs

7 'Duck-billed dinosaurs' is the nickname of which dinosaur group?

a) sauropods
b) hadrosaurs
c) stegosaurs

8 Prehistoric shark *Cretoxyrhina* is nicknamed 'Ginsu shark' after:

a) a brand of very sharp knife
b) a speedboat
c) a ferocious dog

39

Mega mammals

The first mammals lived alongside the dinosaurs but after the great reptiles died out, many more mammals evolved. Some grew to enormous sizes.

1. This is a woolly mammoth. Did people ever ride them?

2. *Basilosaurus*, a giant prehistoric whale, had two little:
   a) blowholes
   b) legs
   c) ears

3. *Castoroides* was a giant beaver the size of a modern:
   a) wolf
   b) lion
   c) polar bear

4. Which of these was NOT a real prehistoric mammal?
   a) giant aardvark
   b) woolly rhino
   c) walrus whale

(5) This prehistoric big cat, named *Smilodon*, probably hunted its prey by:

a) chasing it down over long distances
b) hiding, then jumping out at it
c) digging a trap for it to fall into

(6) *Megatherium*, an elephant-sized sloth, had such huge front claws that:

a) it could dig a burrow the size of a house
b) it had to walk on the sides of its feet
c) it could kill its prey with one swipe

(7) *Chalicotherium* had a face like a ...., claws like a ...., and walked like a ....
Fill in the blanks with these words:

a) sloth   b) horse   c) gorilla

8) *Glyptodon* was a prehistoric mammal with a rounded, bony shell the size of a small car. What are its closest living relatives?

a) turtles
b) rhinos
c) armadillos

9) Gomphotheres were prehistoric elephants with tusks shaped like what?

a) spoons
b) shovels
c) corkscrews

10) One of the largest meat-eating land mammals of all time was *Arctodus.* It is commonly known as:

a) The long-tailed lion
b) The wide-mouthed tiger
c) The short-faced bear

11) Most scientists think that whales evolved from what?

a) sharks
b) crocodile-like creatures
c) hoofed, dog-like animals

12) Irish elk were enormous deer that lived thousands of years ago. How wide could their antlers grow?

a) 1.8m (6ft)
b) 3.6m (12ft)
c) 5.5m (18ft)

40

Dino discoveries

(1) Teeth are the most commonly found fossilized dinosaur body part.

True or false?

(2) In 1947, *Coelophysis* fossils were discovered in New Mexico, USA, with the remains of what inside their bellies?

a) prehistoric crocodiles
b) their own young
c) rabbits

(3) How many millions of years old are the oldest dinosaur fossils yet discovered?

a) 65   b) 125   c) 235

(4) The first dinosaur fossil to be found was of a:

a) *Tyrannosaurus*
b) *Megalosaurus*
c) *Stegosaurus*

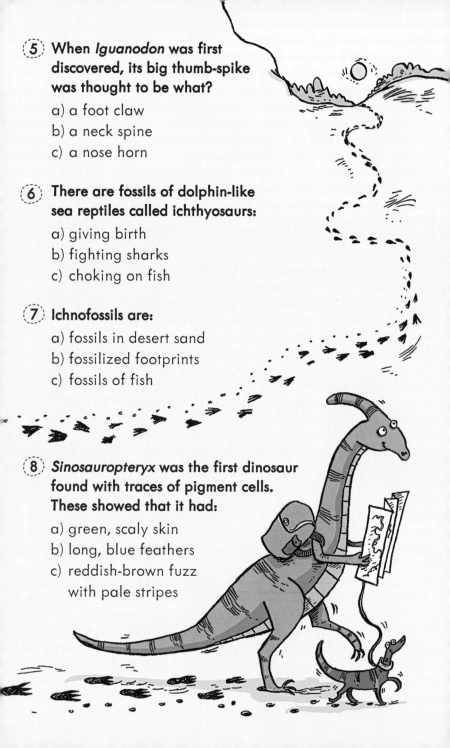

5) When *Iguanodon* was first discovered, its big thumb-spike was thought to be what?
   a) a foot claw
   b) a neck spine
   c) a nose horn

6) There are fossils of dolphin-like sea reptiles called ichthyosaurs:
   a) giving birth
   b) fighting sharks
   c) choking on fish

7) Ichnofossils are:
   a) fossils in desert sand
   b) fossilized footprints
   c) fossils of fish

8) *Sinosauropteryx* was the first dinosaur found with traces of pigment cells. These showed that it had:
   a) green, scaly skin
   b) long, blue feathers
   c) reddish-brown fuzz with pale stripes

(9) A hadrosaur named *Rhinorex*, discovered in the USA, is remarkable for its big:

a) nose

b) eyes

c) teeth

(10) In 2014, scientists announced a new discovery about the giant meat-eating dinosaur *Spinosaurus*. What was it?

a) it was really a plant-eater

b) it spent most of its time swimming in rivers

c) the sail on its back was really a camel-like hump

(11) Which is NOT a true fact about an amazing pliosaur (short-necked sea reptile) fossil found in Australia?

a) it was made out of semi-precious opal

b) it was the largest pliosaur ever found

c) it was nicknamed 'Eric'

(12) What was so incredible about the *Brachylophosaurus* hadrosaur fossils discovered in Montana, USA?

a) they all had six legs

b) they had sharp teeth like meat-eaters

c) they were almost perfect 'mummies', preserving skin and organs

41

Making fossils

All the information we have about prehistoric life comes from fossils. Fossils are the remains of plant and animal parts that became stuck in something that turned hard, such as sand that hardened into sandstone.

1. Coprolites are fossilized:

   a) teeth   b) droppings   c) scales

2. Which is it more common to find fossilized in amber (hardened tree resin): a lizard or an insect?

3. Can vomit become fossilized?

4. Is there more chance of something becoming a fossil if it is buried quickly or if it is buried slowly?

5 Which is more likely to contain a dinosaur fossil:
   a) rock that was formed in the ocean
   b) rock that was formed on land
   c) rock that was formed in a swamp

6 Can eyes become fossilized?

7 Fossil bones are slightly radioactive.
   True or false?

8 A fossil has the same shape as the original object, but is chemically more like:
   a) bone
   b) rock
   c) mud

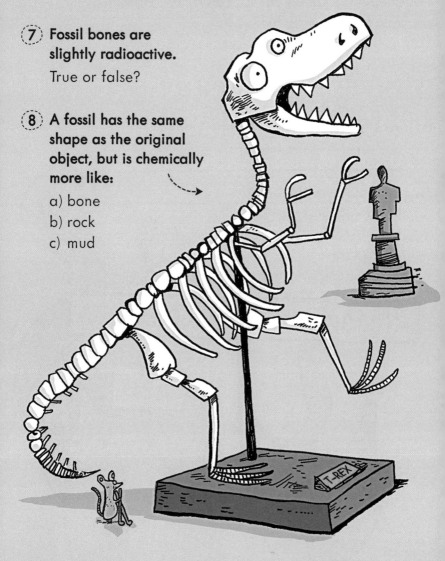

42

Record breakers

1. The longest dinosaur teeth ever found belonged to a:

   a) *Velociraptor*   b) *Diplodocus*   c) *Tyrannosaurus*

2. During the time of the dinosaurs, 5m (16ft) long *Koolasuchus* was the biggest:

   a) amphibian   b) worm   c) spider

3. The oldest known .... made by dinosaurs were discovered in southeastern Australia in 2009. Which of these words fills the blank?

   a) nests   b) burrows   c) footprints

4. *Micropachycephalosaurus* has the longest name of all the non-bird dinosaurs.

   True or false?

MICROPACHYCEPHALOSAURUS

MEI

5. **This is the widest dinosaur. What is it called?**
   a) *Ankylosaurus* b) *Pentaceratops* c) *Stegosaurus*

6. ***Mussaurus* was so small it could sit comfortably in a person's hand. It was the dinosaur with the smallest:**
   a) eggs   b) teeth   c) skull

7. ***Tyrannosaurus* had the biggest dinosaur brain.**
   True or false?

8. ***Kosmoceratops* is the dinosaur with the most horns and horn-like structures. How many did it have?**
   a) 5   b) 8   c) 15

43

Extinction

Dinosaurs and many other types of animals went extinct at the end of the Cretaceous period when a gigantic asteroid collided with the Earth.

1) **When was the asteroid strike that ended the age of the dinosaurs?**
   a) 6.5 million years ago
   b) 65.5 million years ago
   c) 655.5 million years ago

2) **Heat from the asteroid strike briefly set the whole world on fire.**
   True or false?

3) **What is the only type of dinosaur that survived the asteroid strike?**
   a) sauropods
   b) hadrosaurs
   c) birds

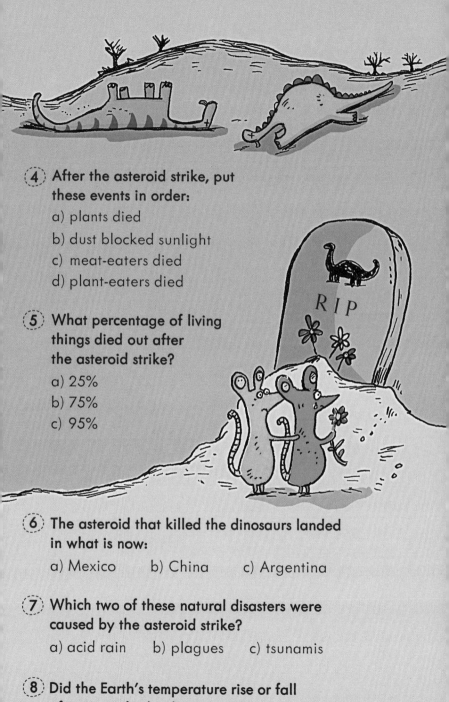

4) After the asteroid strike, put
these events in order:
   a) plants died
   b) dust blocked sunlight
   c) meat-eaters died
   d) plant-eaters died

5) What percentage of living
things died out after
the asteroid strike?
   a) 25%
   b) 75%
   c) 95%

6) The asteroid that killed the dinosaurs landed
in what is now:
   a) Mexico   b) China   c) Argentina

7) Which two of these natural disasters were
caused by the asteroid strike?
   a) acid rain   b) plagues   c) tsunamis

8) Did the Earth's temperature rise or fall
after it was hit by the asteroid?

44

Myths and legends

1. Stories of which legendary creatures may well have been inspired by fossils of the early horned dinosaur *Protoceratops*?

   a) griffins
   b) unicorns
   c) harpies

2. Papua New Guinea is said to be home to flying pterosaur-like creatures that glow in the dark.

   True or false?

3. A legendary ankylosaur-like creature named Muhuru is said to be roaming around the jungle in which country?

   a) Mexico   b) England   c) Kenya

4. When part of a *Megalosaurus* leg bone was first discovered in 1677, it was thought to belong to a giant:

   a) bear   b) human   c) bird

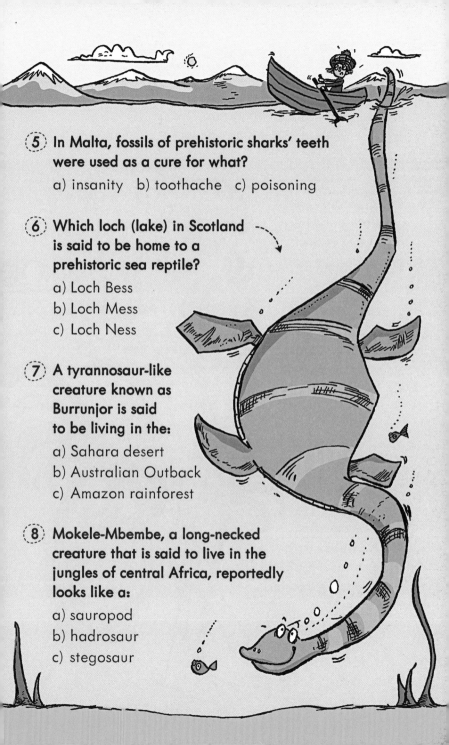

5) In Malta, fossils of prehistoric sharks' teeth were used as a cure for what?

a) insanity   b) toothache   c) poisoning

6) Which loch (lake) in Scotland is said to be home to a prehistoric sea reptile?

a) Loch Bess
b) Loch Mess
c) Loch Ness

7) A tyrannosaur-like creature known as Burrunjor is said to be living in the:

a) Sahara desert
b) Australian Outback
c) Amazon rainforest

8) Mokele-Mbembe, a long-necked creature that is said to live in the jungles of central Africa, reportedly looks like a:

a) sauropod
b) hadrosaur
c) stegosaur

45

True or false?

1. Giant, chicken-like *Gigantoraptor* laid eggs over 50cm (20in) long. To soft-boil one would take 30 minutes.

   True or false?

2. The dinosaurs were a failure because they went extinct.

   True or false?

3. Some prehistoric mammals preyed on baby dinosaurs.

   True or false?

4. The dinosaur *Gojirasaurus* was named after the Japanese movie monster that inspired the 'Godzilla' movies.

   True or false?

5 Sauropod *Apatosaurus* may have cracked its long, tapering tail like a whip.

True or false?

6 The longest complete dinosaur skeleton fossil is of *Tyrannosaurus*.

True or false?

7 The prehistoric snake *Titanoboa* was longer than a London double-decker bus.

True or false?

8 This is *Masiakasaurus*. Its name means 'protruding teeth lizard'.

True or false?

46

Yes or no?

1. Are dinosaur fossils known as 'dragon bones' in China?

2. Did prehistoric mosquitoes feed on dinosaur blood?

3. Did tyrannosaurs store their freshly killed prey in trees, like some of today's birds and mammals do?

4. Could dinosaurs become infested with lice?

5. Did plant-eating dinosaurs pick leaves from trees using their hands?

6. Do dinosaur bones have growth rings like tree rings, that form at the rate of one ring a year?

7. Did any dinosaurs have pot bellies?

8. Were dinosaur eggshells soft and leathery, like lizards' eggs?

9. *Tyrannosaurus* is closer in time to *Stegosaurus* than it is to you.

10. Did dinosaurs normally drag their tails behind them along the ground as they walked?

11. Have dinosaurs ever been in space?

12. Did meat-eating dinosaurs wrap their tails around their prey to catch them?

13. Could small dinosaurs bring their larger prey tumbling to the ground by nipping at their toes?

14. Did dinosaurs living in cold climates migrate to warmer places for the winter?

15. Did *Diplodocus* flick its tail to communicate with other dinosaurs?

16. Were all dinosaurs cold-blooded?

47

Odds and ends

1. **Which dinosaur did some scientists once think had a second brain in its hip?**

   a) *Triceratops*   b) *Stegosaurus*   c) *Deinonychus*

2. **Did all dinosaurs lay eggs rather than giving birth to live young?**

3. **What is the name of the ferocious, spiny dinosaur below?**

   a) *Spinosaurus*   b) *Carnivosaurus*   c) *Ferocisaurus*

4. **Which dinosaur made the longest fossilized dinosaur dropping ever discovered?**

   a) *Tyrannosaurus*
   b) *Diplodocus*
   c) *Argentinosaurus*

5 What is *Brontosaurus* now known as?
   a) *Apatosaurus*
   b) *Brachiosaurus*
   c) *Cetiosaurus*

6 Scientists who study dinosaurs are called:
   a) archaeologists
   b) paleontologists
   c) fossilologists

7 *Diplodocus* weighed as much as:
   a) 1 elephant   b) 3 elephants   c) 10 elephants

8 This duck-sized dinosaur is called *Mei long* which means 'sleeping dragon' in Chinese. Why?
   a) its fossil was in a kung fu pose called 'the sleeping dragon'
   b) its fossil was discovered with its head tucked under its arm
   c) the dinosaur was small but as fierce as a dragon

9 After a dinosaur's shoulders, arms, and enormous claws were discovered in 1965, it was named *Deinocheirus*, meaning 'awe-inspiring hand.' When more complete fossils were found, what type of dinosaur did it turn out to be?

a) a huge tyrannosaur
b) a pot-bellied ostrich dinosaur
c) a lumbering stegosaur

10 Which dinosaur scientist shares their name with a nursery rhyme character?

a) Peter Piper
b) Jack Horner
c) Margery Daw

11 Which dinosaurs are thought to have had the longest lifespans?

a) long-necked sauropods
b) tank-like ankylosaurs
c) 'raptor' dinosaurs

12 US president Theodore Roosevelt once wrote that it was a pity the long-necked dinosaur *Diplodocus* had gone extinct, because:

a) he'd like to ride on it
b) he wanted one as a pet
c) he'd enjoy shooting it for sport

Answers

1 **What are dinosaurs?** **1.** a **2.** c (the other period was the Cretaceous) **3.** b **4.** no (prehistoric sea reptiles aren't classed as dinosaurs) **5.** c **6.** c **7.** b

2 **Tyrannosaurus rex** **1.** c **2.** false (a number of dinosaurs were bigger than *T. rex*, including *Giganotosaurus*) **3.** c **4.** b **5.** false (there are at least a dozen members of the tyrannosaur family, such as *Tarbosaurus*, which looked a lot like *T. rex*) **6.** b **7.** b **8.** c **9.** b **10.** b **11.** excellent eyesight **12.** false (they were strong enough to pin down prey) **13.** a

3 **Sauropods** **1.** a **2.** a **3.** true (they thought that sauropods would have needed water to support their huge body weight) **4.** b **5.** false **6.** c **7.** b **8.** c **9.** b **10.** c **11.** *Dreadnoughtus* **12.** a **13.** c

4 **Diplodocus** **1.** b **2.** longer **3.** b (boa constrictors often grow to 3.5m (11.5ft) long) **4.** true (scientists think this helped it to rear up on its back legs while feeding from trees) **5.** a (it had pencil-like, blunt teeth that it could use like a garden rake) **6.** c **7.** a **8.** in herds (many *Diplodocus* fossils have been found in groups)

5 **Ceratopsians** **1.** c (it might have used its horn to stab at predators) **2.** bone **3.** b **4.** true **5.** b **6.** larger **7.** true **8.** *Medusaceratops* (it was named after a monster in ancient Greek mythology that had snakes for hair)

6 **Triceratops** **1.** a **2.** two **3.** b **4.** b **5.** b and c **6.** b **7.** b **8.** true (the position of holes found in *Triceratops* frills makes scientists think this is very likely.)

7 **Stegosaurs** 1. b 2. a 3. no (they were heavy with stocky legs, so would only have been able to take slow, short strides) 4. no (their plates weren't strong enough and didn't cover enough of their bodies to be useful as protection) 5. bone 6. b 7. true (although the most famous, *Stegosaurus*, did not) 8. c

8 **Stegosaurus** 1. b (It was so named because its plates were first thought to cover its back like tiles on a roof) 2. false 3. no (its back legs were twice as long as its front legs) 4. a and c 5. false (all Stegosauruses had four tail spikes) 6. a and c 7. a 8. b

9 **Dromaeosaurs** 1. a 2. the claws on their toes 3. some may have hunted in packs 4. true (a type of dromaeosaur called a *Troodon* had the biggest brain compared to its body size) 5. b (*Saurornitholestes* may have hunted in packs, or one dinosaur may have chewed on a dead pterosaur.) 6. c 7. false (dinosaurs were very intelligent for reptiles, but not as intelligent as dogs)

10 **Velociraptor** 1. yes, some scientists think they used this method to attack prey bigger than themselves 2. jagged 3. *Velociraptor* (*T. rex* had a bigger brain, but *Velociraptor*'s was bigger compared to its body, which is a better measure of intelligence) 4. no (fully grown, they would have been no more than waist-high to a human adult) 5. no (they wouldn't have been able to fly) 6. c 7. a 8. no (their claws may have been sharp enough to puncture the skin, but not to tear muscle to pull out the intestines)

11 **Ankylosaurs** 1. no 2. c (it was named in 2007, after the release of a series of successful movies based on his book) 3. yes (*Euoplocephalus* did) 4. b 5. false 6. Some scientists think it produced a lot of gas when it ate. 7. b 8. c

12 **Hadrosaurs** 1. a 2. their tails 3. true 4. yes 5. a (they may have used their crests as wind instruments, forcing blasts of air through them to make sounds) 6. a 7. true 8. b

Pachycephalosaurs 1. c 2. b 3. no (compared to their bodies, their brains were not very big) 4. b 5. c 6. b 7. a 8. c

Early birds 1. no (most did, but some, such as *Confuciusornis*, had toothless beaks) 2. false (it was found near Bullock Creek in Australia) 3. b 4. for diving (it could hardly move on land) 5. a 6. b 7. b 8. b 9. c 10. c 11. a 12. b

Dinosaur names 1. after King Arthur's legendary court, Camelot 2. c 3. false 4. a 5. because it looked like a devil 6. a (it's so named because the people who first found an *Irritator* fossil added plaster to it to make it look more impressive, irritating the scientists who had to spend a long time undoing the damage) 7. c 8. b 9. *Triceratops horridus*, *Velociraptor mongoliensis*, *Diplodocus longus* 10. a (the knife-shaped teeth found with it are now thought to belong to a meat-eating dinosaur) 11. b (it was named after the parrot-like 'borogoves' from the poem 'Jabberwocky' in 'Through the Looking-Glass') 12. true 13. b

 Dinosaur giants 1. a (the size of this giant dinosaur is based on a single fossil bone that has been lost since it was discovered in 1877, so some scientists think that *Amphicoelias* never actually existed. If it didn't, then there are other contenders for the title of biggest dinosaur, such as *Sauroposeidon* and *Argentinosaurus*.) 2. *Allosaurus* 3. *Spinosaurus* 4. b 5. a 6. c 7. a 8. c

 Tiny dinos 1. c 2. false 3. c 4. yes (*Bambiraptor* was discovered in the USA in 1993 by 14-year-old fossil hunter Wes Linster) 5. c 6. c 7. c 8. b

Meat-munchers 1. b 2. plant-eaters (only 30–40% were meat-eaters) 3. yes (they had to be more intelligent to find ways to catch their prey) 4. yes 5. injured meat-eaters (hunting other dinosaurs is more dangerous than eating plants) 6. no (all meat-eaters had curved claws) 7. c 8. false (most had four)

Plant-eaters 1. c 2. b (when it was discovered, it was the only dinosaur known to have front limbs longer than its hind limbs) 3. b 4. no (apples didn't evolve until after dinosaurs had become extinct) 5. a 6. yes (they could have used them to fight off attackers) 7. c 8. false (they ate pretty much everything!)

20 **Eggs and nests** 1. a 2. c (they were laid by a giant plant-eater called *Hypselosaurus*) 3. no (they varied in shape from round balls to long, thin ovals) 4. false 5. c 6. b 7. some were covered in wrinkles and bumps 8. true

21 **Babies and youngsters** 1. b 2. a 3. b 4. true 5. a 6. a 7. no (a young tyrannosaur named *Tarbosaurus* had weaker jaws than its parents, so it could only bite small prey)

 Walking and running 1. they walked on their toes 2. false 3. a 4. meat-eaters (they needed to be faster so that they could chase their prey) 5. a 6. true 7. false 8. *Gallimimus*

 Fighting dinos 1. no (but they probably did fight each other one-on-one, and may have hunted prey in gangs) 2. yes (most clawed meat-eaters would have pinned their victims in place with their claws whilst attacking them with their teeth) 3. yes (some scientists think that a dinosaur with large thighs called *Brontomerus* used its big legs to attack predators) 4. true 5. c 6. true (a fox-sized dinosaur called *Heterodontosaurus* had long tusks) 7. no 8. no (*Stegosaurus* had died out by the time *Tyrannosaurus* had evolved)

 Dinosaur world 1. a (Triassic) is the oldest, and b (Cretaceous) is the most recent 2. a 3. false (there is no evidence that oxygen level made a difference to their size) 4. c 5. b 6. b 7. true 8. c

25 **Head to head** 1. true 2. false 3. no (although it used to be thought that some sauropods did) 4. b 5. true (it's *Colepiocephale*) 6. b 7. b and c 8. true

26 **Terrific teeth** 1. true 2. c 3. false (most had just one type) 4. for gnawing plants 5. false 6. b 7. no (some whole groups of dinosaurs, such as the bird-like ornithomimids, had no teeth) 8. *Astrodon* means 'star tooth', *Troodon* means 'wounding tooth', *Deinodon* means 'terrible tooth'

27 **Neck and neck** 1. b 2. false 3. true 4. b and c 5. no 6. false 7. false (the sails wouldn't have been very flexible) 8. true

28 **Arms and legs** 1. c 2. b 3. a 4. abelisaurids 5. a 6. c 7. false (plant-eaters were usually larger, so needed more muscle to carry their heavy bodies around) 8. yes (sauropods did)

29 **Just claws** 1. no (they might have, but there's no evidence to suggest that they did) 2. on its toes 3. no 4. b 5. no 6. c (it might have done this to reach the insects inside) 7. a 8. a

30 **A dino's tail** 1. true 2. c 3. bs 4. c 5. true 6. attract a mate 7. b (it is thought to have used it as a rudder when flying) 8. b

31 **Skin, scales and spikes** 1. a 2. dry skin 3. c 4. b 5. a and b 6. a 7. no 8. softer

32 **Look-alikes** 1. feathery, like a woodpecker's 2. false (it was so named because its fossils were first found on a South African farm called Kangna Farm) 3. b 4. b 5. ichthyosaurs 6. false (it was so named because the name of the mountain in China where its fossils were first found means 'horse mane') 7. b 8. a

33 **Dinosaur family tree 1.** b **2.** yes **3.** false (it was found near the Popo Agie River in Wyoming, USA.) **4.** a **5.** a and b **6.** a (it's so named because it's likely to have eaten amphibians) **7.** c (the archosaurs that were ancestors of crocodiles had a different ankle arrangement from the ancestors of dinosaurs and birds) **8.** b

34 **Walking with dinosaurs 1.** c **2.** no **3.** b **4.** false **5.** a **6.** b **7.** false (Komodo dragons evolved about 4 million years ago, 61 million years after the dinosaurs became extinct) **8.** b

35 **Australian dinosaurs 1.** false **2.** c **3.** c **4.** b (*Australovenator* was found near Winton, Queensland, where Banjo wrote 'Waltzing Matilda'.) **5.** c **6.** c **7.** b **8.** b **9.** b

36 **Flying reptiles 1.** c **2.** no (baby pterosaurs could fly naturally, soon after hatching) **3.** soft **4.** no (they were probably covered in a layer of fuzz, and had scaly feet) **5.** b **6.** c **7.** *Pterodactyl* (*Pterodactylus* was the first pterosaur discovered, and many people use the word 'pterodactyl', but scientists prefer the word 'pterosaur' because it more clearly means winged reptiles in general, not just *Pterodactylus* species) **8.** b **9.** false (many pterosaurs were able walkers) **10.** c **11.** c **12.** true **13.** c

37 **Sea creatures 1.** no **2.** b **3.** b **4.** a **5.** b (many sea reptiles bore live young rather than laying eggs) **6.** a **7.** false (they died out before dinosaurs evolved) **8.** a **9.** b **10.** a **11.** c **12.** b **13.** no (it was about half as long as a blue whale)

38 **Nicknames 1.** a **2.** b **3.** c **4.** c **5.** b **6.** c **7.** b **8.** a (it was given this nickname because of the sharpness of its teeth)

39 **Mega mammals 1.** no (there is no evidence that they did) **2.** b **3.** c **4.** a **5.** b **6.** b **7.** *Chalicotherium* had a face like a horse (b) claws like a sloth (a) and walked like a gorilla (c). **8.** c **9.** b **10.** c **11.** c **12.** b

40 **Dino discoveries** 1. true 2. a 3. c 4. b 5. c 6. a 7. b 8. c 9. a 10. b 11. b (*Umoonasaurus* was small for a pliosaur.) 12. c

41 **Making fossils** 1. b 2. an insect 3. yes 4. quickly (there's less chance of it being eaten or decaying before it can become preserved) 5. b 6. yes 7. true (they give off radioactive particles, but not enough to cause any harm) 8. b

42 **Record breakers** 1. c (the longest tooth found so far is 30cm (12in) long) 2. a 3. b 4. true 5. a 6. a 7. true 8. c

43 **Extinction** 1. b 2. true (it is thought that rock pieces blasted up into the atmosphere, then fell back as a burning rain that cooked the planet, setting plants alight and roasting anything that couldn't hide underwater or underground) 3. c (most scientists believe that birds evolved from the group of dinosaurs that included *Velociraptor*) 4. b, a, d, c 5. b 6. a 7. a and c 8. it fell

44 **Myths and legends** 1. a (there are many *Protoceratops* fossils near gold mines in Mongolia's Gobi Desert where griffins were said to live, and they do have beaks and four legs) 2. true 3. c 4. b 5. c 6. c 7. b 8. a

45 **True or false?** 1. false (it would take 2–3 hours!) 2. false (the dinosaurs lasted for 165 million years; humans have only been around for about 1 million) 3. true 4. true 5. true (computer simulations show it could have done this, perhaps as a warning signal) 6. false (*Diplodocus* has the longest skeleton) 7. true 8. false (it means 'vicious lizard')

46 **Yes or no?** 1. yes 2. yes 3. no 4. yes, some scientists think that lice would have lived in the feathers of some dinosaurs 5. no 6. yes 7. yes (therizinosaurs did) 8. no, they were crisp and brittle like hens' eggs 9. no (*Tyrannosaurus* lived closer to our time than to the time when *Stegosaurus* lived) (continued overleaf)

46 Yes or no? (continued) **10.** no, they normally waved them in the air **11.** yes, *Maiasaura* and *Coelophysis* fossils were taken into space on NASA space shuttles **12.** no **13.** no **14.** yes, sauropods and hadrosaurs are likely to have migrated short distances to warmer climates **15.** yes, some scientists think that it used its tail in this way **16.** no (scientists think that some dinosaurs could keep their body temperature warm even if their surroundings were cold)

47 Odds and ends 1. b **2.** yes **3.** a **4.** a (it was 44cm (17in) long) **5.** a (after the first *Brontosaurus* fossil was found and named, it was discovered that this fossil was actually an *Apatosaurus*) **6.** b **7.** b **8.** b **9.** b **10.** b **11.** a (scientists think that the biggest dinosaurs probably lived the longest) **12.** c

With thanks to Simon Tudhope and Michael Hill

First published in 2015 by Usborne Publishing Ltd, 83–85 Saffron Hill, London ECIN 8RT, England.

Copyright © 2015 Usborne Publishing Ltd. The name Usborne and the devices 🌂 👑 are Trade Marks of Usborne Publishing Ltd. All rights reserved. No part of this publication may be reproduced, stored in a retrieval system, or transmitted in any form or by any means, electronic, mechanical, photocopying, recording or otherwise, without the prior permission of the publisher. UE.